made of
earth

Typeface: Rachel Irving

Graphics provided by: Good Studio

Designed by: Alisha Christensen

ISBN: 9798792023833

here's to you:

the ones who keep loving
despite having every reason
not to.

I'd tell you that this is a work of fiction, but that would be a lie. Based on true events. Some details and timelines have been changed. Hope you hate it.

contents

made
of earth

where she grows

the womb

it started when I was in the womb.
soaking in resentment. I guess I cannot
blame her for that. maybe I burned her
insides and fire came spilling out of her
lips when I came tearing out of her hips.
maybe it was hard to see where the love
is when you've taken all she can give.

the crow cries over these
quiet suburban streets
dry summer heat
palm trees and
jasmine growing by the front door
playing in the flower bed
lining up the snails
like seashells on the shore

notes from California

my mother didn't much like bugs, but she
didn't tell us that. instead, she would point
them out and say, *"well, would you look at
that!"* like she was fascinated by the slimy
things - the creepies and the crawlies
she never touched them
but would tell us, *"pick it up!"*
she didn't want us to be afraid of them
but maybe we should have been
maybe I would have some sense of
self-preservation
but I don't
and I should
for some reason, wasps always land in my
hair every summer at least once
half the time I don't even realize that
they're there until I brush them out with
my fingers and find them in the palm of
my hand
looking a little lost and confused
me too
sometimes I look back and wonder
if she saw me like she saw the bugs
necessary
but a nuisance

insect

it's raining again
this time it is welcome here
like the warmth of my gram's hands
on my shoulders
her musky Chanel goes perfectly with
the gold chain she wears around her neck
and that hint of lipstick on her lips
you'd never know they kept secrets
locked up tight, but maybe that's where
she got the sparkle in her eye
the shine isn't just light
it's also fight

*we don't talk about it

the sparrow was a gardener of sorts
she grew herbs and berries
built a fence with hedge
to keep her flowers in
some flowers she would water well enough
to watch them bloom
bring them in and
set them on the windowsill
look at what I grew
others she'd forget to tend but
they still found the sun and
she would bring them in and
set them on the windowsill
look at what I grew
and some she'd rip up from the roots
not a flower
just a weed

the sparrow comes to my balcony
every summer morning
as long as there are sunflowers
and yesterday I watched her
pluck off the petals
and leave them on the street

silly me.

I thought she came to eat

she was an empty ghost
just like the flowers
she'd drain of their sweet
watching nectar drip down their limbs
just so no one else could taste it
sitting on her throne of bones
made from the wings of those free birds
who flew too high
too loud
too fast
she would rather watch you drown
wearing her pretty little crown
while you're gasping at her feet

I will let the sun kiss my back
where you left your scars
did you think I didn't hear your words
carried through the walls?
the echo hit my chest then came to rest
between my ribs
seeping through the bones and
finding their way in
leaving your jealousy
tattooed on my skin
where love
should have been

there was a time
when I trusted you
was there ever a time
when you trusted me?

one day your daughters and sons
will hear the lies rolling off your tongue
how will you explain it to them?
how can you tell them
that you know what love is
when you cannot speak the truth?
why would they believe you?

he is nine and he is wise
he has eyes and those eyes
see truth
and he isn't afraid to speak it
repeat it
believe it
even when older eyes
that are not as wise
try to hide their lies in honey
the truth is not as sweet
as they make it out to be

I don't know how to ask for forgiveness
because what I said is true
and you'll tell me it doesn't make it okay to
say but it didn't stop you from doing it
the difference is that you expect me
to be silent
and I won't
and all the good times
don't make up for all the
  I'll give you a reason to cry
  You could have had my parents
and you don't see that I still do

if these lungs could eat
they would swallow you whole
bones and all
then spit out your teeth
instead of holding my breath
the way you never hold your tongue
when you speak

I have filled my body
with so much water
but still my mouth and lungs are dry
this is what it is to be
the daughter of a wildfire

unquenchable, never satisfied

they say how can you talk about your
mother that way
she gave you breath and
she can take it away
but what they don't hear is the truth
you kept yours hidden behind the doors of
our home while I spoke out and said
well actually
that isn't true
then you sit on your throne letting
I love you's fall from your lips
like you actually mean it
and maybe you do
maybe this is what love looks like to you

you're so much like her
they'd always say and I'd smile
be polite and say
thank you
when it really made my stomach curl
please no
not her

like mother, like daughter

you and I've been
breaking bones since we met
hard to love but
both desperate for it

Dear Father,

I heard you read my poetry and that you're disappointed. Again. You can't believe that I would drag my mother through the mud like I did. I laughed when I heard this. You can't believe what *I* did? I can't believe that you stood by for years while your lover used her words like a battering ram on my body. I can't believe that you're disappointed in me when it was you who pulled my sister's hair because she didn't agree. You who went to the basement screaming because your boy loves boys. You who beat us naked with a belt, beat my brother's legs until they bled, then tell us that you love us after it. I know your father did the same, that his father probably did too, and even the men before him, but you didn't have to. I hope the pages burned your fingers as you read them.

no wonder we were drawn to the ones
that hit and spit
it wasn't just a bad decision
or poor taste in men
this is the way you told us love is

there is a river in the canyon where we
used to go with fishing poles and old worn
boots. I almost caught a fish once. My
father was disappointed when I lost it and
I realize now it was disappointment in a
lost experience to teach his daughter
something about fish and not
disappointment in me because I didn't
catch it. But I didn't know the difference.
And I think I've been searching for
approval since.

my father told me
that I was all the best qualities
of he and my mother
I didn't believe him then
and I don't believe him now
because if that were true
then how
and why
don't you take responsibility
for the rest of me?

you gave us knives and taught
us to fight - so why are you
surprised   when   we   do?

*standing up to you

do not tell me to speak gently
when you cannot do the same

what is it like to be so
disappointed all the time? aren't
you starving? how are you not
groaning bones by now ... I guess
you've been feeding on
insecurities for so long you do not
know the difference between
living and alive.

There was this one time I was mowing my grandpa's lawn. He tried to make me do the dishes because I am a girl, but I hate the dishes. I'd rather mow the lawn so I trade jobs with my brother.

"He will do the dishes", I say and I walk out the side door through the garage to the mower.

My grandpa hands me a green trucker's hat to put on my head, so I do, but as soon as he leaves I take it off. I want to feel the sun on my face and hats make me sweat and you can't feel the breeze.

So I'm mowing the lawn while my brother does the dishes because it's 2000, not 1950, and I see a tiny snake slithering in the grass.

I gasp from delight and probably also to catch my brave, but I am not really afraid of snakes. If you grab them just right they can't bite.

So I snatch up the slippery thing and run to
my father because I want to show him how
wild and brave his daughter is. *"Look!"* I say
and hold out my hand and he steps back and
yells,

"get that thing away from me!"

I catch my breath surprised because I
thought this man was afraid of nothing.

So I take the snake down to the creek
and let him go
and this is the first time I know
that I am stronger than my father.

*uncaged daughter

the second time I know
is when I stand up to her
and you demand that I apologize
but why
I was not wrong and I was not rude
what I said was simply true
so I don't
and I won't
and you tell me I
    cannot leave this house until you do
so I cancel my plans and tell my friends
I won't make it tonight
and if pride is a sin
I like the taste of it

Today is his birthday. I don't know how old he is anymore. Old enough to know better, that much is true. And part of me wants to hold the boy that you were and say, "I'm so sorry you didn't get the love you deserved from your father." The other part of me wants to stay safe, so I burned the bridges I kept constructing out of false gods, fake smiles, and desperation for your approval. And you can drink up your disappointment in me like I drink up mine in you and I hope one day you'll know what a spine feels like. Because I do.

your photo popped up in a memory today
we were smiling, spines straight
I look so much like you
and you look so happy, so proud of me
and I could feel the burning in my throat
the aching in my chest
I wasn't expecting it to hit me like it did
because it's not like that anymore
I'm thirty-three
it shouldn't matter to me
and somehow it does
but it's not worth the compromises
the false pretense I would have to dress in
to give you that again
so I won't

when I was eighteen I used to break open
the back door around midnight
leave the windows unhinged just in case my
father woke up and checked the locks on
the doors like he sometimes did
I'd walk slowly down the hollow streets
past the house where they sold weed
past the house where they did harder things
past the firefighter's house
to the house across the street
from the elementary school
through the back door
that opened to the laundry and a woodshop
turned left to the kitchen
right to the hallway
then left to climb into his bed
sometimes we'd just lay there
and it was nice to be someplace where I
was wanted even just for an hour or two
then I'd leave
walk slowly down the hollow streets
crawl through my parents' bathroom window
and back into my sheets
trying to convince myself
that I was wanted here too

My first kiss was my brother's best friend
but he was also mine

he and I were in a spiral staircase in a turret,
like a castle, but they called it a tabernacle
it later caught fire and burned halfway down

it's a temple now
holy, I guess
or maybe the devil in me brought her
tumbling to her death

I suppose we'll never know

But it was quick and awkward and electric
like most first kisses are
a whole fifteen seconds of, *oh my god*

a few days later when my parents asked me
if I'd kissed anyone lately I lied and told
them no

I should have known that they already knew
someone saw us holding hands at school
and gossip runs like a river through these
streets like the ditches carrying the
irrigation water we still played in - seeping
into the neighbors yards and into the ears of
the gossip whores who couldn't stop
drinking it up

I guess it was delicious to the taste and I was
made into Eve after just one kiss
forbidden to see him

like that's ever worked in the history of ever
it just makes you want it more and I got it
be sure

I let his fingers dance all over me and
the clergy heard about this and
he told the parents and the parents told
their friends and their friends told the
others and my *sins* kept circulating in the
streets like the ditches carrying the
irrigation water we still played in

silly children

didn't anyone tell you
that water will make you sick?

standing in the middle of the chapel on a wintery
Spring day. the end of March, like a lion.
snow and rain outside at the same time -
slush in the streets

I was eighteen ... you must have been forty-three or
a little older and you're screaming at me because
I said I didn't want to take your diaper bag to the
car outside - I would take it to my class instead

and I'm watching your face turn red while I'm
running through the last five minutes in my head
trying to figure out how we went from
preaching Christ-like love
to this
how we went from mother-daughter
to rivals
I didn't ask for any of this
I was never competition
so why did you make me a competitor
you threw me into the ring from the moment my
lungs could breathe and I don't even know why
you realize I had to fight you my whole life to
stay alive, right?
but I can't take the tirade anymore and my
tongue can't speak anyway so I drop everything
and leave
go out into the slush-covered streets even though
I just said I didn't want to but I want to get away
from you before I cry so I grab my keys and open
up that old 80s Pontiac
it has a bench seat and I like that
it's comforting for some reason

but   it   doesn't   stop   my   heaving
heavy   breathing
or   the   grief
clouding my eyes.

I start the car and start to drive away and my
father - your husband - pulls into the parking lot
at the same time that I'm pulling out and he asks
me,   *are*   *you*   *okay?*

I look at his face and think, *do I look like I'm*
o   *k*   *a*   *y*   *?*

he looks the same as the day he found me crying
on his bed, and this time I don't lie, but can only
shake my head. I think he tells me to be safe as I
drive away and I find it strange that I find
comfort sleeping on an old bench seat in an old
car in an old parking lot across town than I do in
my own bed.

do you remember what happened next when I
came home?

now I'm sitting in the middle of my apartment on
a Spring-like Winter day in January, like a lion.
I'm thirty-four ... just a little younger than you
were and I have only been a mother for ten years
but I still don't understand what I did to deserve
it.

what I do know
is that I didn't.

do   you   remember?

the   day   you   told   me   to   leave
"submit"   or   pack   your   things   and   go

do   you   remember?

when I came home and you were eating
dinner, guests at the table, and you still couldn't
help yourself. opening your mouth as soon
as I opened the door, asking *where have you
been!* like you never left without saying a word

I remember their heads bowing, not in prayer
like I'd seen before, but in disbelief. they were
seeing a side of you that I had always seen

do   you   remember?

I turned to leave. got one, two, three, four
steps out the door when you came out
s   h   o   u   t   i   n   g
then grabbed me by my hair and pulled me back in

maybe   that's   why   I   started   cutting   it

do   you   still   blame   me?

I   know   what   you   said   about   me   then
-   have you learned from it? because I did

44

there is a grumbling coming out
the cave. a low rolling tumble then
c   r   a   c   k
like a tree snapped in half.
back   away   slow   -   beware
- we do not feed the bears

he comes because he says
he is worried about me
but he tells me

you need to perform your wifely duties

> (I won't have sex with someone I
> don't want to have sex with. My
> body does not belong to him and
> giving my body away when I don't
> want to feels worse than any *"sin"*
> I've participated in)

just pretend he's someone else

> (then what's the point?
> I may as well leave now)

is this about someone else?

> (no, it's about me and my body and
> how I feel - having sex when I don't
> want to with someone I don't want
> to makes me feel like dying)

if you just orgasm you'll like it

(that's not how it works)

he could be getting sex
from anyone at his age

(so could I and
I told him he could
if he wanted to)

well, this is pretty selfish of you
to tear apart your family based on sex
you have no reason to complain
now that you've taken church out of the
equation it makes it so much easier,
doesn't it?

(silence)

I tried

(so did I)

he comes because he says he is worried
about me but this man is not my father
and he tells me

think about your covenants
think about your children
what will this do to them and
your eternal family
I love him and your father

        (but do any of you love me)
        (listen to what I am saying)

I come to her
because I am worried about me

     (help me stay married
     because I don't want to be.
     I feel like I'm dying)

*well, you'll just have to figure that
out. people are sexually attracted to
strangers, as* you *know, it's not that
hard to figure out.*

they gathered around her
held her up, kept her fed when she left him
they tell me, it's different, she tried
and he hurt her all the time
you have nothing to complain about
stop being selfish
you brought this on yourself

I watch you - your lips speaking
words over mine. did you ask me a
question to have a conversation or so
you could run your own lines?

I let you speak for me so
long I lost my voice

* i n t e r r u p t e d

god is not consent
marriage is not consent
coercion is not consent
guilt is not consent
my body is not a reward
a hobby
or a cure
this is what you should have told me
I am not a bag of flesh
holding my insides and his
dripping down my thighs
no one asked me what I like
if I was okay
just told me I had a job to do

perform your wifely duties

I step into the rain
rinse
like I can peel the depression
from my skin

do you smell that
  smell what
the boxwoods
they smell terrible
  what do you mean
  I don't smell anything
you don't?
they reek
  I think they're pretty
I can't stand them

                  then I remember
                  that boxwoods
          were the fence that kept us hidden
                      and to me
                  they smell like anxiety

nothing feels right at the end of July
no one knew that a few days later you'd be
lying in the ICU hooked up to tubes and a
machine that kept you breathing

and now I count August by fives
one
it's your birthday
five
it's a hospital bed until
ten
we're driving home and get the text
fifteen
why are we smiling at a funeral
twenty
wake me up, please tell me I'm dreaming
twenty-five
put on a smile so by
thirty
everything looks fine
but it isn't

nothing feels right at the end of July
because I know what happens next

I make love to myself
in my apartment on the couch

you want to hear about that
but not how I was bleeding out on this same
couch remembering that my sister is dead
but I literally never forget

there was that one time in Georgia when I
was cleaning her pan and I wasn't sure how
to take care of it; stainless steel and all so I
picked up my phone to call her and ask

I looked up to tell him what I'd done
and   he   looked   at   me   and   said

that was dumb

It had only been a year and ten months
can you blame me?

and when that two-year mark came
I was coughing up boulders

god, they're so heavy

and he asks, *why are you* so sad *lately*

and I tell him
maybe
because it's the anniversary of her death

and he says
so?
like a question

and I regret not tearing out his throat
my skin on fire because he still has a voice
breathes this fucking air and he has never
lost anyone he cares about as much as he
cares about himself

I lost my *sister*
the sun
who showed up every morning
every goddamn day
for everyone
including you

so?

I should have known
that I could never come back from that

she is the one
who showed me how to be alive
how to love and how to be kind
how love is more than just saying so
it is showing up when it is inconvenient
it is saying no and enough
and tell me more
about the things I do not understand
love is more than your expectations
and my obedience

they say you never die
but is it true
because I can hardly feel you anymore
did I shut my heart too tight
maybe
but I had to
because it would still be dripping red
and I still don't think you ever get over it
death, that is
the scars heal but they're still there
phantom pains like your phantom eyes
they say you never die
but is it true

tonight I was in the kitchen singing and dancing while making dinner and thought about how you'd have been by my side through this divorce just like I was with yours, but I ended up doing most of it alone, except for those few and they know who they are. and I heard your voice in mine when I hit that melody and ended up crying on the kitchen floor ... but kitchens were made for dancing you always said and tonight they're holding my tears instead.

they cut down the magnolia tree by
your grave. what a foolish thing to do
- cutting down the most beautiful
thing in the cemetery. and I suppose
it's no different than what we do
when things become too beautiful to
hold.

her tongue is dry and
her hands are crestfallen with dirt
she needs water
a valley full of it
why are you coming back to cut the grass
can't you see she is burning
let her rest

god is coming home soon
be ready
be better
he's always watching
I've lived half my life afraid of dying
wary of not just the men in the streets
but the one in the sky
they say watches over me
a vengeful god
one who watches children like me
be thrown into pits and burned
sacrificial lamb
like it's respect, not slaughter
watching his sons and his daughters
cry out from the dust
this is someone I'm supposed to praise?
supposed to trust?
they say god is love--

                              show me his hands then
                                    that is blood

        *the god I knew

they always ask why
why did you leave
give me all the reasons and then they try
and tell me all the reasons I should have
changed to stay
nevermind that I folded and corroded
rusting in my skin 'til you could see the
bone to fit somewhere I didn't belong
anymore
believe me, I tried
I've been kneeling my whole life to gods
I could never satisfy
shapeshifting
cracking ribs and dislocated limbs
an eye for an eye
but just pulling out mine
all for blood
be less, they said
so I was
but it would never be enough

I dare you to stay

here you are again
circling over my body
waiting for a corpse to feed on because
you like the taste of rotting flesh
watch it falling from your lips when you
speak of me
if you have to talk me down
chew me up and spit me out
to sit up on your throne
then your crown is nothing more than
stones that will break your fragile wings

if my womb could weep
she would scream out about the bones and
raking fingers that touched her
they take
without so much as a breath of hesitation
or those without an ounce of imagination
or intimacy
jackrabbit between our thighs and
they wonder why
we'd rather go to sleep

I wonder what you used to look
like before. who cracked your
earth open for the first time -
was it the quaking or the river?

what people don't see is the aftermath
the hesitation
holding your breath
like you wish they'd mind their business
they never asked about you before
but now
they can't keep your name off their lips

she is swallowing your lies with her
mariposa smile - knowing that lies
only last so long before the truth is
given wings. before the others see
your tongue covered in blood from
the ones you chewed up and spit out
to line your golden-colored streets
and if looks could kill you softly,
well - she'd take you from the knees.

I wish I was a kinder woman
but I am not
I hope my spirit sends you trembling
like cockroaches shrieking
when they see the light

I will make you
a bed of nettle leaves
so you can feel
the sting you gave me

do I miss you
of course I do
well
I miss what we could have been
when will you see
that I'm part of you and
you're part of me
whether we like it or not

do you think writing about you is easy?
it's exhausting
then you'll ask me why I do it
and sometimes I don't know
I just want it to go away
and writing seems to help not just me
but them too
so yes
I write about you
but what was it you always said?
> *the world doesn't revolve around*
> *you. stop acting like it.*

and maybe this is why
I don't understand humility
was it supposed to be humiliating?

my toxic trait is convincing myself
that the people who truly love me
actually don't. and maybe this is
because my mother would tell me she
loved me but didn't know why and
then she'd leave. so I just believe that
when men tell me they love me,
they're lying. and sometimes it's true;
they love me, then leave. I think
sometimes we just keep chasing the
love we knew.

I wonder if you had loved me better
would I stop searching for love from
empty men. trying to fill my empty
womb where you ripped me out and
left me on the ground. a thirsty
weed. trifling little thing. bitter like
my roots.

unearth / rebirth

I am not ready to have a man in my home. I don't know where his hands have been or if they can be trusted. how well did you love the ones before me and do you still? are they a memory that makes you happy or one that makes you relieved? do you know the difference between love and jealousy? can you make a fire that keeps you warm without burning the whole forest down with your insecurities? do your hands grow flowers from their fingers or do your weeds linger at the throat?

if you do not know how to be alone
then I don't want you in my home
you do not get to fill your ego with my
body just to fill your bones

I like my men made of sunflowers
and a little bit of rain, but they carry
their own umbrella and use their
hands for love when the thunder
comes instead of using it for their
fists

I do not want a man who runs on adrenaline like addiction. I do not want a man at all if he cannot be at peace with his demons or admit that he has them. we all do. I do not want a man who cannot face his pride or a man who lies because he does not know what truth tastes like. I do not need a man who is whole, but I do not want a man who breaks branches and bones to say, look at what a sad, lonely man I am - no thank you - I've had enough of that and I've cleaned up enough broken bones of my own.

hands are the first thing I notice in a man
because hands tell stories his lips can't
or won't
lips tell secrets
lips tell lies
but hands can't hide

and maybe this is why
I'm drawn to the men
with blackened knuckles
the ones that smell like
smoke and gasoline
because dirty hands mean
they've had to work for something

*the first place I look is the palm of your
hand* - the mount under Mercury - the one
that holds the healer's mark. so far none of
the men I've had have carried it. then I look
at your thumbs - they show your self-control
your ability to understand and speak about
your temper. sometimes they tell me to run
and I still don't hear them. then I look at
the creases and crow's feet you carry - how
deep do they go or do you have none - it is
always unnerving to see smooth hands - a
calm canvas - mine look like glass right
before it shatters. then I find your eyes and
ask about your mother . your father . your
family . does your voice change when you
speak of them - do they taste bitter in your
mouth - is there mercy on your breath - *did
you get the love you needed so you do not
take mine from me without any intention of
giving it back* - tell me your greatest regret
- the last person who meant something to
you - the last time you cried and why - then
I go back to the palm of your hand and
decide if I want to hold it.

give me a man who is water first - fire, air, then earth. because water cools my fire and his fire caresses my rain in a way that makes my shoulders smolder all the way down to my roots until only embers remain and his breath breathes them back with an autumn summer kiss because a man made of earth is too heavy for my chest.

set in stone

that night I was trailing my fingers over
the candlelight shadows on my thighs
slow dance to a firefly sunset
and a hibiscus moon
I didn't know these hips were calling you in
but I'd do it again

I put jalapenos in my tea
molasses in my coffee
and garlic in my honey
I guess I like it sweet and spicy

waking up
drinking coffee on your balcony
surrounded by trees
while watching the sea
make love to the sand
watching them dance
like lovers in a tangled tango

romance

I watch the way you love everyone so easily - never questioning who is deserving. it comes so naturally and I wonder what it's like to love like that. I have so much to learn from you.

tonight I went out to the plains and
stood in the rain while the thunder
shook the ground and kissed my
skin with its dark grey clouds and I
watched the lightning dance in
ribbons of white and purple lips
pulling me into the dirt and into his
hips

a desert flower
thirsty for a drink
dirt caked at the knees

I want you
like the earth
drinking up the rain in June

it is Sunday morning
and I am drinking caramel coffee
covered in cream, like most days
but today it is raining
a gentle thunder serenade rumbling like
the way your whispers danced over my
body like butterflies in the sea and
I'm sipping on my caramel coffee
covered in cream
wishing it was your lips

I want to marry you in yellow
white has never been my color anyway
purity, submission
I am none of these things
I am yellow
the color of my dress coming undone
and the sunset coming down
a halo on this crown
full moon coming over the peak

and when I say *marry*
I mean combine poetry and the art of living
your body and mine
you as you are and me as I am - we -
no churches
no preachers
just woodsmoke and a vow

that I will love you as well as I love myself

this morning I woke up to the moon
and the sky was pink and purple and
blue - calling you at five-thirty in the
a.m. do you remember last summer
when we stayed up all night and neither
one of us wanted to say goodbye so we
didn't - even though you were thirty-
four and I was thirty-three
we had responsibilities and you told
me that it wouldn't happen again
so I drank up everything you would
give me
god, we were thirsty
and ten-thirty turned to five then you
said goodnight and I watched the sky
turn from pink to purple to blue
just like this morning
when I woke up to the moon

I know you're coming back
you always do
but I don't know if I even want you anymore
you were my dream
everything
until he touched me again
and why would I want you
when I could have him?

I   run   through   men   like
w   *i*   l   d   f   *i*   r   e   s,
they say. I don't want to burn
you down.

I haven't seen you in seven years
and here we are
your lips touch above my eyes before
they ever meet mine and I know it's not
your intention, but I can't help but push
my hips into yours
I want every part of me
touching every part of you
I could lose myself right here
in your lips
but you take my hand
like you always do and show me all the
things that have made you *you*
parade me around the room but not to
say, look at this trophy I carry with me,
but look at my queen
you are not afraid to show you love me
publicly and for the first time in my life
I am proud to call a man mine

are your eyes grey or green? I can't seem to place it. You tell me they are green and I should know this because the men with green eyes always pull me in. and you joke that maybe I am colorblind but maybe, your eyes are making me nervous with the way you keep taking me in like you're watching a stormy summer sunset while smoking a cigarette. it's not the same as the men on the street who undress me with their eyes and even though we are both naked in this bed your eyes are on mine. oh my god, it makes me nervous. I can barely look at my eyes in the mirror for longer than it takes to apply my mascara and you are drinking me in like it's the first time you've tasted the moon. and you tell me to stop looking away but I have never had anyone look at me for so long with so much tenderness ... like you are planting wildflowers with your lips. you see me. and your love is filling me up so quickly that I'm afraid my skin will break open and you will see that I am nothing but weeds.

I want to write about him
but I don't have the right
he was only mine for one night
like we were making up for all the lost
years and now we're sitting here drinking
beers in the living room
naked on the couch
what would our parents say
if they could see us now?
when they ask how I am tell them
I am the best you've ever had

you're sitting there
wearing nothing but your guitar and
you start to play
it looks so easy
effortless
like a steady rain
and I can't stop staring
and I say, *that's sexy*
you laugh and say, *but we just had sex*
but I can't stop watching the way you play
and now I understand
how your fingers move like they do

I want to write about the way you
touched me and made love to me, but I
don't because I am selfish. I don't want
anyone to know how well you love. How
you put a crown on my body and
worshipped me and all of my mountains
and valleys. How you brought a peridot
rain to a sardonyx desert and my
sardonic sway. How you made me soft
around the edges from the moment I
tasted the cigarettes on your lips again.
I've always loved the way you taste
even back when I was seventeen,
nineteen, and now thirty-three. the way
you love(d) me is healing.

my sister was a prodigy
my brother did art
but I was just pretty
so when you say
you're so fucking smart
it's my favorite thing about you
that's when I know that I
am in love with you

remember when we went out that night
and your brother got in a fight and my
parents said that it wouldn't happen again

(but it did)

you tasted like cigarettes and a good time
with your hands all over my body in a
parking lot at ten o' clock
because they said
nothing good happens after midnight

(but what about before?)

you'd meet me downtown
we'd run around
dancing all night 'til we burned out then
we'd make out underneath your porch light
those were my best nights

I've got this memory of you in Long Beach
underneath the avocado tree
when we were three

(or four? I don't remember anymore)

but I knew then you were my best friend
hold me close don't let me go

life moved on so we did too
but I'd always come back to you

and when we were nineteen
you told me
you loved me
and I left you there like I didn't care
because I knew I was no good for you
then I moved away, had some babies too
and after leaving him I found you

now we're thirty-three and you tell your
friends about me
mine say I've never looked so happy

I meet you downtown
we run around
dancing all night 'til we burn out
then we make out
underneath your porch light
you are my best nights

I want to know what you think of me
do I rattle your bones
when you wake up in the morning
do I slip in your thoughts
when you're talking to her
am I still the best thing
you have ever tasted on your tongue

your voice is like
a steady rolling thunder
gentle and audacious
like you know I can't resist it

I <u>want</u> to hear from you
I'll always be into you

shouldn't sound like poetry to us
but it does because we don't hear
it enough

one night was all it took to fall back in love
with you and driving home through the
canyons I asked for a sign like I always do
grabbed myself a coffee
smiling at the sunflower
in the vent of my car
the one I picked from outside your building
growing wild in the parking lot
then the sun came tumbling out of the
clouds and there it was
my double rainbow
I never told you about it because I know
you're not the type to believe in signs even
though you love that I do
so when you sent me that photo with a
double rainbow outside your building
over the sunflowers growing wild in the
parking lot and say
I think it's a sign
I can't stop smiling because it's true

I want late nights with you
dancing in the kitchen
like we used to dance downtown

when you tell me that you love me
I believe you
because it comes from your roots
when we're standing in the living
room and not your lips
when your head is between my
thighs

we're at a bar about to leave
when two men smile and
invite us for a drink
both with skin like mine
blended melanin
one with dark braids and a flat brim hat
one with a nose
that reminds me of my grandfather
he says *you're spiritual aren't you* and I
smile because he sees me
I ask where they are from and they tell me
Long Beach
and there is an instant connection
an explosion of stars or deja vu because
that's where we were born
but our families moved away when we were
four and they tell us
it is probably better that way
and I wonder who we would have been
if we'd stayed

they called us a cute couple
with *"your different skin tones"*
and the word "couple"
makes me cringe inside
not because I don't like it, but because it's
touchy terrain
you don't deny it
but you don't confirm it either
I can tell it made you squirm
felt it lay heavy on your brain and
I should have known what was coming next
too much
too soon
too real
too good

(here we go again)

hand in hand
breath for breath
the lungs
the throat
the head
the heart
our sweat
with a cautious crescendo and we
melt into the night then
I stay awhile and love you
can I trust you to love me

before the wind blows I want to
pick up your old tired bones and
take them home then put them on
my shelf next to my old tired
wings and the both of us together
are really something aren't we

how can I love you, the sun asked the moon
you are so far away
you can't, they said,
just let me be a sad and lonely thing
they kept her at arm's length and more and
she tried to share her warmth but they
turned their back
said *I don't need that*
and still the sun held the moon

you know what's beautiful?

men who aren't afraid to love you openly
men who say, I want you to tell your friends
about me and I want you to meet mine
men who recognize that you are a living
breathing being and can witness your
happiness without trying to tear it down
because it makes them feel weak
to see you smiling
men who see your insecurities without
feeding them to keep you hungry and heavy
men who do not go searching for lips to fill
with their own
men who can sit in silence alone
and still feel whole
men who are not afraid to cry because they
know that their tears are better healing
and divine than the brave they've been
expected to put on their face

men who keep reaching for the sunshine
men like you

I want to lay on a mossy rug in front
of a hedge wood fire. my body draped
in a little bit of moonlight and a velvet
throw. a drink in one hand and poetry
in the other. and you're there too - a
cigar in one hand and sage in the other.
I can feel you in my chest. I am not
afraid of loving you. of being loved *by*
you. it's like you and I share roots.

I don't want to tell you that I love you
because I don't want to put that on you
and I don't want to be the one to fall if you
feel nothing at all. So I put my words in a
chokehold, don't let him know what we
know, but I know you know. You say come
out to the west and we play fairytale pretend
and act like this is love. I go home and bury
all the daisies and all the things I'm feeling
lately because I don't want to be the one to
fall if you feel nothing at all. So I put my
words in a chokehold, don't let him know
what we know, but I know you know. Then
I'll write poetry about you and act like I
don't fucking love you because I don't want
to be the one to fall if you feel nothing at all
because I do.

I don't want to take up too much
of your time, but I want to give you
all of mine.

it's not that loving me seems unlikely
it's the distance
what will we do with that
which one of us will uproot their life for the
other and is it fair to ask
fair to tell you that I would leave here if my
flowers didn't have the roots that they do so
I can't dig them up and leave for you
and you cannot pick up a building covered in
gold and I wouldn't want you to anyway
but how can we make this feeling stay

I want to open up my jar of secrets
sprinkle them like salt
in every conversation
to see if you like the way it tastes
is it too much too soon
I already know that I'm in love with you
but could you be in love with me
with the three of us

you tell me that my little
wolves are fierce and wild and
I smile because I am their
mother. where do you think
they got it from?

I may have a butterfly's tongue
but I am wild as they come

show me the ones who made you
feel like you were hard to love and
I will show them how well you love
me. that we are not broken ... merely
buried under an endless blue sky
that never holds the rain, but I hold
yours and you hold mine and that's
the kind of love I like.

there is something delicate about you
like you're standing at the edge of the forest
with a match in your hands and it's not like
you want to burn the whole place down but
you don't know how to let go without lighting up
and I just want to be
someone you trust
someone you love
someone who loves you enough
for you to see that you are safe
here with me
I love you
and I'm in love with you
and I wish that was enough

my insecurity is starting to leak
I want you
but do you want me

rain, rain come this way
and maybe keep me company
hold my drink
tell me that you love to hear me sing
because I'll believe you
and I know my voice will keep you

a hummingbird
came to my flowers today
but I moved too quickly
and scared him away

I know it is easier to run
than stand here in this love
but please try

I'm used to the ones I love leaving
or tearing up my insides with an
I love you, for now
until you fuck it up again
and we all know you will

did I love you too well, too quickly
was my nectarine tongue
too sticky sweet for your skin
leaving you to crawl out of it
before you could taste it
did I love you too well, too quickly
licking the cobwebs from your body
that you left there for years
did I love you too well,
too quickly, my dear?
come, my love
let me do it again

August is fading and part of me
wants to wrap a lasso around the
stars and hold time right where we
are. but it comes back kicking and
screaming to be let out, so the rope
burns my hands and I have to let go.
I think letting go is the hardest part.
letting go feels like losing, and I've
already lost enough.

I wish I could give you more than
dirt. but the ash is all I have left
after being burned for so long.
do you know how much time it
takes for the forest to come alive
again?

there is a spring in the mountains
where I go to undress and dip my
toes in its aquarian caress while
the sun sets slow in a purple-pink
glow with the water rippling up
my spine and up to my neck
f   o   o   l   i   s   h
I don't have an Achilles heel
I   have   an   Achilles   head

how easily I let this love slip
d   r   *i*   p
down   these   canyon   walls
as   if   it   never   existed

I don't mind the solitude. truly.
but once I get a bit of you on my
tongue I am starving. I want to
wear you down to the bones.

I love being alone so well that you cannot
forget to show me that you love me
I don't need you
I never did
I chose you
again
please don't make me regret it
I am not someone
who will beg for your attention
I do not chase
I get indifferent
and indifferent
is like closing the door behind you
then realizing you lost the key
so, please
if you love me
show me
I am not an afterthought kind of love
and if that is enough for you
do us both a favor and leave

I want to be
    unreachable
    untouchable
    unfazed by the silence
but all I want is for you to
    (reach me)
    (touch me)
    (love me)
I hate the way I come so easy
when you finally open *your mouth*

there is a fine line
between medicine and poison
and my darling,
I can't tell which is you

why am I like this
everything was fine before I thought about it
thought about you
I can even do the casual sex
but it's the romance that gets me
then I don't hear from you for days and it
starts chipping at my crown until I take it
down and put it on my shelf next to my old
tired wings / why was I wearing this thing in
the first place?

(you don't really love me)

but where is that coming from
and why am I so desperate for it - the love -
and why can't I hold it?

I can only tell you exactly what I
need so many times before I
realize that you won't make the
time. Only so many replies that go
unanswered. I've already done
this. And it's not worth it.

I know I can be a mad one
cross me once and I'll come straight for blood
I guess I learned it from my mama
but you kind of like the wild ones
you take my hand, you call me *lady*
and you say loving me is easy

but the trouble with love is
it's never enough and
you had no intention of keeping it up
you tell me you love me
but you don't know what that means
tell me how you sleep at night knowing what
you did to me
and tell me why I stay

I know I can be a hard one
I fall too far and I expect too much
I guess I learned it from the poets
but didn't think about their broken hearts
you kiss my lips, you call me *lady*
and you say loving me is so easy

but the trouble with love is
it's never enough and
you had no intention of keeping it up
you tell me you love me
but you don't know what that means
tell me how you sleep at night knowing
what you did to me
and tell me why I stay

now I'm dancing on my own
holding bottles and my phone
trying to let you go

but I know you can be a mad one
they cross you once
and you'll come straight for blood
I guess you learned it from your father
and I kind of like the wild ones
you look my way, you call me lady
and you say loving me is easy

but the trouble with love is
it's never enough and you had no intention
of keeping it up
you tell me you love me
but you don't know
what that means
tell me how you sleep at night knowing
what you did to me
and tell me why I stay

you said loving me was easy
so tell me what's the trouble?

and *I love you* seems more like
goodbye - a groan from the
beasts we carry on our backs
we're tired of saying things we
don't mean. but we don't know
how to quit.

the   thing   is   I
don't   want
b   *e*   *t*   *t*   *e*   *r*
I   want
y   o   u
even   for   worse

do I only crave the things I cannot
have? why does the wanting taste
so delicate - filling me up like I was
starving until you came in with a
single kiss as if I was a senna living
in the desert and this drink would
be enough to last me.

thirsty

my, my, my
what have we here
a lonely little raven and
a late October chill
three
four
five
they say
you'll never come out alive
six
seven
eight
they'll be waiting at the gate
nine
ten
but ain't the devil handsome

good grief.
you   wouldn't   know   love
if it hit you in the teeth

are   we   lovers
or just friends that fuck
when   you   bury   your
bones   inside   me
is   it   love
or just enough to keep
you   going   -
and   do   you   think   it's
enough   for   me

they   all   want   a   taste
there's   something   about   a   wildflower
the   way   she   moves
the   way   she   sways
delicate dancing daisies in a summer rain
but they can never hold the thunder
so   they   run
every   damn   time
when   will   I   learn
they're   always   lying

people always look for someone to
replace the one who got away
instead of being the one to stay

I thought I could trust you
to love me well
well
at least better than the rest
but I guess I'm only good for one thing
when it comes to love
and that's leaving

I had never seen a rattlesnake in my
whole life until that night with you
on the mountain under the full
desert bloom thunder moon. if I had
known then what I know now about
how nature gives us signs ... I would
have left you that night.

he made love to me too, you told me without
blinking and it didn't hide the sly in your
smile. I sighed wondering why you think I
would give a damn ... did you forget that I
was the one who left this man? I was the one
who said no. I was the one who ended things
and he was the one who begged for me. so he
made love to you too. good. I hope it heals
you both.

what is it about a woman's naked body
that make the men go mad?
what if I told you
it is not the woman's naked body
but the man's need to devour everything
because his own flesh is empty

it would be different
if you left me for *you*
but leaving me
for another human being?
that never works
believe me
or better yet
believe the men
who have already done it

I don't want to write about you
but I do
so I can get your body off of my chest
your tongue off of my lips
pull you out of my hips
get you out of my head
and out of my bed
and I don't want to write about you
but I do to forget

isn't it foolish
that I still care about you after you left
how casually you made me a casualty
how I still want to keep my body to myself
just in case you want it back
naive
it's not like you're holding on to me
you've moved on
while I'm still here hoping
I guess maybe I just want to say
I love you
one more time
I didn't know that the last time I was in
your bed was really the last time I was in
your head as someone you wanted to love
you introduced me to all your friends
told me you loved me when I left
then started leaving me on read for days
remember how I told you
at the very beginning
it's okay if you change your mind
just don't fucking ghost me
then you did
how did I already know that would happen
and why did I stay
and why do I still want to
how do I let go of you

You left. Typical. They always do as soon as they come inside you. I guess it's hard when two stars collide. And I wish I could reach up inside my womb and scrape out the insides and throw them in the dirt so you aren't there anymore . . . watch the cracks drink you up like they drink up the rain. Let it grow flowers from the nostalgia and the heartache.

Instead, you're in my skin where your fingers touched. In the lining of my lungs where your breath met mine before our lips ever did. You're in the necklace I wore. Those tangled stars like our tangled bodies tangled around my neck. and I don't regret doing any of it. I regret that it ended like it did. Because I didn't just lose my oldest love. I lost my oldest friend.

Actually, I really wanted you here. I
wanted your hips in mine, your lips on
mine. But more than that was the
pleasure of your company. Your time.
Then your voice became an echo of all
the men who could have loved me
well, but didn't. And I don't think you
meant to lie to me like you'd been
lying to yourself, but I know now that
I loved you too well for a man that
cannot stand in his own skin.

I made a home for myself in this body
you were supposed to come gently

you knew about the beasts I carry
you weren't supposed to leave
your mark on me

men come to me for healing
I lick their wounds clean
stitch up the seams with soft fingers
seal them with a kiss
love them until their tears run clear
then sing them to sleep
and they thank me

no one has ever loved me
like you do
you changed me
you showed me
I love better because of you

and I know
then I'm back on my knees
gathering up the stardust
they emptied from my bones
left so carelessly
scattered over the floor
trying to pour it back into myself
but it keeps spilling out

healers need healing too
I thought that could be you

why should I care
and how do I stop?

*loving you

made of earth

you knew better
than to love me like you did
did you think before you started
peeling back the layers of my skin
but you like the way I tasted on your tongue
did I make you come alive again

they always leave and tell me
 I hope you find a man
 that makes you happy
 someone better than me
but I was never looking for a man
to make me happy
I am happy without one
honestly, sometimes happi(er)
without trying to keep them fed
so let me be clear
I allowed you to love me
I let you into my life
I won't make the same mistake twice

I'm tired of men loving me
just enough to fuck me
leaving me for another garden
just to come crawling back
when they realize
they missed out on the best thing they had

without intimacy all I am is a body for their
own fantasies

I want to fuck your pretty little face
stick it down your throat 'til you choke
I like it better shaved
I want you to get on your knees
show me
more

but if you'd asked me - then you'd know
that   I   want   you   to   undress   me

s   l   o   w   l   y

but don't touch - breathe over my chest
while you're moving your hands over the
hills and valleys of my body - heat pulsing
between your palms and my skin before
you put your lips on my throat and open
me up like you're touching a flower for
the first time

those soft pretty blooms coming for you

p   u   *l*   *l*   u   *l*   a   *t*   e

then we can talk about what you want

they are always surprised
when my tongue comes whipping out
it has not always been sweet
I had to learn to come gently
but I am tired of being the lesson
I am not the remedy to your aching
I will spit the poison out
into your own mouth
don't give me those eyes
I thought that's what you liked

you don't get to treat me like you
did and still have the pleasure of
my company.

I hope we can still be friends

I bet you do.

they always come back
these men who watched you bloom
then left you to dry
these men love honey
but cannot take the sting

maybe it's me
maybe I don't have the capacity
for a healthy relationship
maybe I fall in love too quickly
my expectations are suffocating
grand gestures aside - what is left?
maybe I'm too high maintenance
do I expect too much text
and not enough sex
but what is sex without connection
and what is connection
when you're not here
so I guess I'll just go watch the sun set
because he's always there

letting go is usually easy for me
I know that most people are
temporary. that's not a self-fulfilling
prophecy, it's just a natural thing.
most people are not meant to stay
but you?
you are not a makeshift love
you are a mountain climb
limb over limb to watch the sunrise
you are the places I visit
not just once, but twice or more
because once wasn't enough
you are late-night drinks while
watching me dance then pulling me
in close and kissing
my hand
my head
my hair
and holding me so hard
that it hurts to let go
and letting go
is usually easy for me but

you are dirty hands
bad habits
deep regret
tough shit and tenderness
        you are
        fiercely
        madly
        wildly
        perfectly human
and you are everything
I love about living

*alive

I have a gift for you -
she held out her hand filled
with seeds. plant them by your
front door in the spring. they
will remind you to be happy
and when you hold the blooms
you'll remember how you used
to hold me.

how do I take this insecurity
and let her fall gently
without her thinking that we still
have a chance to be together again
yes
there is someone else
it's me

dear god,

it's been a while. I haven't missed the old you that much. but sometimes I miss the old me. the one that was so hopeful and trusting. the one who believed you were someone good and that I could be too. the one who found comfort in praying, but the silence got too big and I guess I stopped caring about what you think. I realized my relationship with you was more about my need to please them. and we all know I'm no good at that. Sometimes I still find myself on my knees - in the sand. in the dirt. on the floor at the edge of his bed. these are the only prayers I have left.

there I go again
thinking that he's the one
when will I learn
there is only me
I will not wait
for a man to make me holy

I don't know how to make myself better
when I don't know what made me sick
I wasn't trying to pick a poison
I just wanted a sip from the bottle
now I've got them lined up
taking shots
looking for the remedy
like it's not already inside me

let the moon undress you before they touch your lips. never forget what your own fingers feel like against your skin, between your thighs and raking over your ribs. how you made your own breath shake before they ever breathed your name.

*tell them who you're
really coming for*

the remedy

I am not a delicate woman. don't let
my eyes fool you. I do not speak softly
or walk gently - even with bare feet
you'll hear me coming. I swing open
doors like the devil is after me,
because actually, she never left. but
we've made peace for the most part . . .
now that I wear her tongue
around my neck. and I don't trust
bodies even though they trust me
so I carry a fever in one hand
and moonseed in the other
so no. I am not a delicate woman
but I was never meant to be

They said I was made
of monsters
a scorpion sting
in place of a kiss
a venomous tongue
too much
too much
bite your lip
the devil's desert daughter
dressed in black
deathstalker; both life and death
bury me in the water
they say I'll carry you to the dark
but have you seen the stars?

*dance with me

let me tell you about these hands
that have been digging in the dirt
pulling up roots to brew into remedy
turning   tragedy   into   medicine

once there was a girl and she was made of
earth and she grew into a woman with lips
made of butterflies and thighs made of
thunder and she was gentle like water
fearless like water
wild like water
calling down the rain
waking up the green
and she grew daughters
and sons and everyone in-between

her fire was an ugly beast
a hungry, thirsty, bellowing thing
devouring the living and the dying
and that's the thing no one is willing to do
carry the corpses
they all want to taste the bed of roses
dripping with rain
from those delicate golden lips
run their fingers down her willowy limbs
and pick flowers from her fingers without
getting their hands dirty

and her fire brought life to the earth
that had died - consuming the flesh
and the parasites no one else wanted
to touch - making way for the
sunlight to kiss the ground and
breath air into the earth's rib cage.
these lungs cried out as they tasted
the salt-kissed wind for the first
time and her breath made clouds in
the sky and the clouds brought rain
and the rain fed the earth and the
earth held the fire that brought life.

she holds the sky on her spine
and the earth in her chest
carrying them s l o w l y
across the starlit sea to the shore
never asking for anything more or
less, just holding the sky on her
spine and the earth in her chest

she had healing in her hands
and drew her medicine from the dirt
she drinks from mountain rivers
and sleeps in salty seas
made from salty tears falling
onto salty lips
dances in the rain
magic moving from her hips
with a mane made of moonbeams
eyes made of stars
still growing wildflowers from her scars
and she will pick them one by one then
give you seeds to bloom
because this is what healers do

I'm trying to forgive you
and it's hard, but seeing how
the light in your eyes has
died now that you don't
have mine makes ripping up
these weeds so much
sweeter.

take your tears tonight
go into the garden and
follow the old woman
dressed as a golden spider
she will show you
how to gather up your weeping
and weave it into
the marrow of your bones

her   bones   grew   roots   and
these   roots   grew   trees   and
the   trees   called   the   flowers   and
the   flowers   called   the   bees
and   the   bees   made   honey   and
the   honey   came   with   sting
but   that,   my   love,   is   life   you   see
and   the   sting   brought   the   rain   and
the   rain   held   the   dirt   until
the   dirt   made   mud
and   the   mud   kissed   the   skin   where
the   hurt   was   holding   on
let   it   go   -   let   it   gone

as soon as it hits 60
you will find me
soaking up the sun
with prickly legs
like prickly pears
airing out my greasy hair
drinking lemonade and iced tea
like it's summer
when it's 60

surviving winter

I've got to be honest
I just want to walk around topless
in the sunshine
cut off shorts and nothing but the wind
on my chest
those rays licking up my sweat
making shadow dancers on my breast
bare chest
like my neighbor walking his dog
down the street in this
eighty-degree breeze
but instead I'll put on this dress
because it's the closest I can get

why am I always wet
my breasts are sweating and
so are my thighs
even my elbows and knees
are dripping in this heat
I thought I was made of fire
maybe that is why I
make so much water
from so much heat with nowhere to go
so my eyes fill up quickly
when I hear a sad melody
a beautiful story
a tragedy
and even when
I'm full of anger with a side of salt
the fire and water collide
so I make islands
for the love to grow on
and maybe that is why I
am made of fire

yes
I have a tendency to undress
strip off my clothes like I strip off
your stuck up nose at the end of
every conversation
I came into the world
with nothing but my
bare
naked
body
and my beautiful
naked
screaming body grew
and bloomed
quick
cover her up
never let her skin see the sun again
cover her shoulders
they're connected to the boulders
that bring men to their knees
please
I came into this world
with nothing but my
bare
naked
body
and that's how I'll leave

do the layers of my skin make you weak
does my open tongue sting you
even when she comes gently
what is it about me
that unburies your ghosts
can you hear their bones
rattling in their graves
I guess they'd like some company
and it's either you or me

she said *I saw you in the waves*
what were you doing there
swallowing salt
don't you know that will kill you
if you take it in enough

how do you heal the womb
wash the roots
soak them in water until they are soft
scrub off the dirt left by careless hands
and thoughtless words
fill the cracks with the tears you choked
back because you thought you deserved it
you did not
chew them up and spit them out
it is yours now
it always was

let the breath settle in your
lungs and grow love between
your thighs. let it soak into your
womb where the others took
your roots. the thunder is your
mother now. did you hear what
she said? you are and always
were the medicine.

let her out kicking and screaming
like the day you were born. we do
not have to die in silence and we
do not have to give you peace
when it was ripped out from under
our feet - the healing is in the
release.

I don't want to hold this anger
it's burning holes in my hands and
I am too full of love
to let you drain me of it again

I hold to my love
like you hold to your grudge

I don't cry anymore
not like I used to
because my body is in peace
not in pieces

I've been holding onto lifelines
scared of the monsters hiding in the dark
waiting for me to fall so they can say

I told you so
there's no way you can be happy
alone

I can feel the tears creeping up
is this the depression knocking at my door
I'm scared of falling into those pits again
watching the sky change from night to day
but the sun never touches me
and it always rains
is this the depression knocking at my door
what are these tears here for
I'm scared to let them out
what if I drown
but these tears are made from relief
not grief
these tears are holding me

*peace

today I am tired. I just want to sleep
and it scares me because is this the
sleep that pulls you down to the deep
sea and keeps you until your lungs
burst? so I keep my eyes open because
when I am awake I am safe and I know
that I am happy even if my eyes are
burning for relief. I just need to sleep
because I am tired. It is just a regular
tired from a whole, beautiful life. So
tonight I will sleep. Come wake me if
I'm gone too long.

I like to sit in the morning sun
drinking coffee for breakfast
while the crow flies solo
to who knows where
but I always wonder where he's going
watching the shadows
dance across my skin
caressing it
these are not the same shadows
that dance on my shoulders
these shadows are made from light

I get tired of trying to prove that I
am worth something to you. in a
world that is so big I lose
perspective.   it's   overwhelming.
why am I trying to be anything?
this is why I go back to the earth
every time. seeing her wide open
makes my eyes open wide and I see
that I am a beautiful kind of
c   r   e   a   t   u   r   e
maybe   even   something   divine

I am finding god after you
leaving the sinner's song at the altar
it's burning my tongue
spitting out the ashes and dust
I lost faith in the bricks that built this
church; the holy houses made of gold
built on worried and weary bones
they say there is only one
but I know
that god is in the mountains
in the sky
and in me
that holy
is getting dirty
showing that your hands are scarred from
lifting heavy things and heavy hearts
I am finding god after you
and she's a loving thing
because god is in the mountains
in the sky
and in me

awakening

you speak of alchemy
as if it is not the same
as your Sunday grace
as if your songs are not the same
as the heathen hymns falling from our lips
with the same reverence as your amen
you will not bury our sacrament again

I hope you find comfort in your god
I hope your god gives you peace
just like leaving him gave me

get   on   your   knees   for   me
such   a   pretty   little   thing
you   hungry   fools
don't   you   see   this   crown
I   kneel   only   for   myself

I bless my coffee before I drink it
and this means something to me
coming from where I did
I let the liquid fill me to my toes
like they said the holy ghost would
I no longer plead to a god to notice me
like I begged you and so many men
and now I find god in my coffee

I come from a line of broken women
like broken rivers singing in a broken song
where the water starts to moan / turns to
mud / turns to stone / and she is left
wandering trying to find her way home
without a map. leaving her feet bloodied
and bruised until she gets tired and picks up
those stones and instead of finding her way
back to the water she turns on her daughter
and says:

> *look at what you made me do*
> *look at this blood on my shoes*
> *look at all you took from me*
> *look at this blood on my knees*
> *look at my broken body*
> *look at me*

she is thirsty without the water ...

I come from a line of broken women
like broken rivers singing in a broken song
moaning for the sun to set yet it doesn't and
she is lost without her map because this is a
daughter whose mother never found her way
back to the water and she was left bloodied
and bruised passing these stones to you

but *daughter*
let me tell you

that life comes even from broken rivers when
you open up your chest and let the rain fill it
and empty it over and over again. these
stones were not meant for your feet or for
putting blood on your knees. these stones are
your way back to the water.

so daughter
carry those stones
bury them in the water
she will make peace with the edges
bottle up the river
carry her around your neck
put her in your pocket as you wander
drink her up
when your mouth is dry
like the earth in July
do not cast your dry spells on the earth you
walk on or the flowers that you touch
it ends here

     enough

you say Eve was a wicked
thing - when you know
damn well she's the Queen

so I'll go to the water
I'll go to the sea
I'm the devil's daughter
but this ends with me

you didn't love me well
you couldn't
you didn't know how
because the love you knew was covered in dust
dirty footprints walking away
they never wanted to stay or say
I'll help you clean it up
when they were the
one who tracked in the mud

you didn't love me well
you couldn't
you didn't know how
because the love you knew
drew lines in the dirt
this is as far as you can go
no more
too much
but still not enough

you didn't love me well
you couldn't
you didn't know how
because the love you knew
left bruises you couldn't see
cunning tongues are good at hiding

you didn't love me well
you couldn't
you didn't know how
to love yourself

I didn't love you well
I couldn't
I didn't know how
because the love I knew was covered in dust
dirty footprints walking away
they never wanted to stay or say
I'll help you clean it up
when they were the one
who tracked in the mud

I didn't love you well
I couldn't
I didn't know how
because the love I knew
drew lines in the dirt
this is as far as you can go
no more
too much
but still not enough

I didn't love you well
I couldn't
I didn't know how
because the love I knew
left bruises you couldn't see
cunning tongues are good at hiding

I didn't love you well
I couldn't
I didn't know how
to love me

cycle

I am a parent. a *mother,* they say.
but I don't feel that way - because I was
raised with parents who expected you to
obey at all times and if you didn't, what
happened next depended on the day and
the child. sometimes nothing happened at
all and I thought it got better after a while
but when I was older I heard about the
things that happened after I flew away and
well - some things don't change.

I come from a generation of fathers and
mothers who trapped the wild of their sons
and their daughters with half-dead hymns
chanting from broken lips. so when they
say I am *a mother* ... I don't feel that way.

if anything, I am a guide: holding their
hands and showing them the light even
when it is very hard to find. or not there
at all.

I am a gardener: planting seeds / pulling
weeds / but knowing that there will always
be weeds. the trick is to learn to grow with
them.

and I hope that when
these little loves grow
they see a mother
who is *whole*
a *wild mother*
with a *wild love*
and when they say
she is *my mother*
I believe them.

and though I am wild and free
what these little wolves need
is a love that is soft and steady
I have to remember
that their love is not measured by how fast
we run or how many trails we climb
what their love needs from me
is soft and steady
so that's what I try to be

sometimes I wonder if I'm hurting my
children in ways I can't see
then I hear him whispering,

> *it's okay, accidents happen*
> *I made a mistake,*
> *proof that I'm trying*
> *I am kind*
> *I will give him ten tries*

and I see them
talking to the bugs
the butterflies
and the flowers
telling them
they're going to be okay

(and so are we)

*healing

here, the woman says. *drink this.* she is holding a mug in her old tired hands. knuckles like tree knobs / rough like tree trunks. *what's in it,* I ask. it looks like mud pulled from under a cypress tree in a swamp. *drink it up,* she says again. so I begin. it is bitter and boiling. it burns as it goes down and I want to spit it out, but I don't and she tells me -

it is made from the tears of your grandmother's mother and her daughters and the ones before her. your grandfather's pride and anger and spite he tries to pass as respect. his sons' split lips and the ones before them. the aching of men who never felt a gentle hand from their father until they fell into another man's arms

it is made from the grief of generations who do not know what their home feels like under their feet / they have never felt the mud between their toes / never seen their mother ocean or heard their mother tongue

it was made from the ones who have never felt tenderness between their knees. they were taken from the womb too soon

it is made from the cries of truth that were
buried as lies from an unsound mind
- they always say the women are crazy -
and their pleas for help they covered in dust

it is made from the broken bones and blood
of every being you came from

she stops. my cup is empty. my breathing is
heavy and my insides are burning. I can feel
my ribs cracking. *what did I drink up?*

she looks at me and says, *most never make
it this far.* then she puts her old tired
hands in mine - knuckles like tree knobs /
rough like tree trunks and tells me

but in it there is also love.
can you taste it?
there is just a little bit of it
but it is there
and it is up to you
to make the next cup.

made of earth

here I am now
made of earth
grown from the dirt
that tried to bury me

the woman with the wild gray hair who
says, *here you go, baby*
as she hands me a pulled pork sandwich
the woman with the gold tooth who says
how you doin' sweetie
then says she likes my plants
the woman who knew my sister
long before she knew me
who still shows up quietly
with love notes
years after she was buried
the grandmother
who reminds me of a willow tree
and tells me I'm doing all the right
things even when it feels like I'm failing

> *the women who don't know
> they're healing me

tell me
what's on your mind
    (I was looking at the butterfly)
my nature girl
the willow smiled

I saw them today
carrying love in their hands
but not for me
but we don't want things
we want parents
who take responsibility
for the messes they made
the tirades
the names
the silence
     (am I still here)
     (do I still exist)
and part of me wonders why
they didn't try with me
there were no gifts
no apologies
what is it about me
that makes you love me differently
I am grateful that this is curiosity speaking
and not the little girl that was so desperate
for your love
I understand that I will never have it
like I want / like I need
I've come to accept that
but I wonder if you see
that you're doing the exact same thing
your mother did to you
and his father did to him
to me

a bronzed and wrinkled shirtless man with
a gaping tooth grin and a tattoo on the
corner of his chest crossed my path as I
walked by with my flowers in hand and
I could see that this is a man where
mothers grab their children and pull them
in close so I make sure that I don't and I
look him in the eyes and we both smile
then   he   practically   yells,
- *b e a u t i f u l b a b i e s h u n* -
his pride is palpable as if he were my
own father. I can feel it pulsing from his
heartbeat - his happiness for me radiates
and I want to wrap my arms around his
leather skin and kiss the cheek next to his
gaping tooth grin because this is all I
wanted to hear from them.

I don't think we ever stop wanting to be loved by the ones who created us. There had to be a little love there in the beginning. For most of us anyway. Maybe we were made from a bit of lust and momentary madness as well. Or maybe we just fell from the stars and the dust got in their eyes ... made them blind to the light they'd been carrying inside them. Maybe we were much too bright for sore eyes. Much too wild for feet that have been standing in one place so long that they bleed because they are so heavy. Sinking because they're not moving. And I don't think we ever stop wanting to be loved by the ones who created us. But I won't let the fear of losing you keep me here.

I hope your love grows
as your flowers do
that you never leave them wondering
if you love their tired wilted petals
just as much as you love
their sunshine summer hues

I hope one day you will be able to say
I love you
without it coming after a sermon
I hope you learn to like the taste
of swallowing your pride
I did it all the time
And maybe one day you can say
I'm so proud of you
when I am true to myself
even when you don't agree
we are still family
and I wish you could see
there's nothing wrong with me and I
am worth loving even with my edges

today my head was full of weeds
dry and dusty thirsty things
so I went to the water
under the moon
in the middle of September
and the water filled my ears
so I couldn't hear you anymore
what a relief

the earth holds me
the way a mother should

what do you think about love
you know, I believe in love and that it can
be beautiful
I always have
but most of the time we get so stuck in
what we think love should be instead of
embracing it and loving it for what it
actually is and love is sometimes really
ugly. not ugly as in fistfights and
disrespect and emptiness and concession
and forcing it to be something it isn't.
but ugly as in vulnerability
the kind that says
here are all of the beastly things about me
will you love me still
sometimes it's pretty boring
and that doesn't mean it's ending
sometimes boring is a season and
sometimes love is just really steady
it doesn't have to have the extremes
it doesn't have to feel like a hurricane
it doesn't have to feel like a tornado
it can be a slow and steady growth
I think love is really beautiful
and I believe in it even after all of the
heartache and failed relationships

I believe that love can be healing
and I believe that love is a gift
I believe that love is more than just the sex
I feel it differently in my chest
the way it sits beneath my breast
underneath and between my ribs
that is the love that I'm seeking
that is the love I've been dreaming of
I believe that love is good
I believe it is possible to have the love you
want and not just the love
that is convenient - but
the love that you crave
the love that fills your belly and your
womb. the love that makes you feel alive
I don't believe that love has to make you
feel caged and used
I don't believe in love until you die
I believe in loving everyday

that's what I think about love

I get tan lines between my thighs where
they kiss. there is no space between my
knees - these thighs made of thunder or the
trunks of trees. I get tan lines where my
belly rolls like hills and rivers, just like it
did when I was little - except now it is no
longer considered darling, more used as a
warning: *this is what happens when a
woman lets herself go* ... never thinking
that *maybe* this body holds the spells of
creation and the prayers of lost children,
lost fathers, daughters, mothers, and sons.
all this body wants is to know peace - not
be a reckoning. and I get tan lines between
my thighs where they kiss. there is no space
between my knees.

my skin is getting old and tired
sunkisses and wrinkles and grey
fixing it would be easy
they do it all the time
but I want to be an old withered tree
these lines by my eyes
my lips
my tired daisy breasts
and hips
tell stories
I would never replace them
chasing the fountain of youth
the secret to immortality is loving so hard
and so well
that the forest will speak of you
long after you're gone

my skin has always been
compared to olives
but I don't like olives
and they are green
my skin only turns green when it is bruised
and if I had to choose how to describe my
skin I would tell you that it came from the
dirt of mountains or the center of a sunset
gloriosa daisy in July
I am copper glittering from the desert sun
in the sky and even when you add mud I
am still shining bronze
not olive green

and I am not something to eat

nothing makes me
love my skin more than
when it is sunkissed in the summer
and I finally see that I am
made of earth
and my ancestors
rise up from the dirt of
my shimmering
bronze brown body

and if you ever wonder
if you skin is beautiful
just look at the trees
they come in all colors naturally
and so do we

how did you come to be
she said to the butterfly
and she began; let me tell you about a time
when I was a hungry little thing
just existing
in my yellow and green and black
and that is where I learned to be
existing as others saw me
never dreaming that I could have wings
even though I wanted them so
I kept taking on the other's colors and
fears and well
they started to bury me, my dear
because you cannot be a happy thing
living for another's reality
so I took the dirt that they threw
on my yellow and green and black
and I made that my bed
wrapped myself up and
rested my head for a while
and filled her with pretty little things
and beautiful dreams
turning that dirt into mud into something
that made me smile
it took some time and yes, it hurt like hell
but I am here to tell you about a time when
I was a hungry little thing
just existing and now
I am living for me

I want to call up my old friends and say, *meet me in the mountains,* so they do. and they bring their kids and we light a fire, cook dinner, and play in the river. we put them to sleep in tents under the stars then stay up half the night under the moon right where we are - laughing like we used to.

*miss you

Find the people who run to the rain and chase the moonrise. the ones who will sit on their car all night and watch the lightning strike then gasp in awe like you do. find the ones who dance bare feet on the concrete. the ones who take too many pictures and love too deep. these are the ones you keep.

this is a recipe for the lonely:

get up. I know you don't want to. do it anyway. open up the windows. you do not live in a box. give yourself feet. I don't care if it's the shower, the sea, the river, or the rain, just get yourself to the water. add salt. find the sun if you can, fake it if you can't. wrap yourself up in the warm, sticky air of a greenhouse, the colors of a kumquat sunset, or sweet pink magnolia blooms. eat something. the coffee, the wine, and his lips don't count. say thank you, even if it tastes bitter the first time. say it again. one day you'll mean it.

I think healing is like skin
breaks open
gets bruised
becomes whole again
it doesn't mean the same skin won't break
in the same place
it doesn't mean you were never okay
some things are here to stay
and some scars never fade
I have a scar from when I was ten years old
on the left side of my knee
I was riding my bike while we were
camping and I slipped
on some slippery rocks
tore my leg up
a three-inch swath of blood
like someone took a dry paintbrush and
left just one stroke of poppy red on the
sidewalk but the sidewalk was my leg
and today I am thirty-three
that scar didn't fade
it's still there on the left side of my knee
some things don't heal pretty

I hope one day it stops hurting
that one day the aches
stop burning holes in your chest
that one day you can look back on this
your patchwork skin
and feel stronger in it

I hope you stop standing in places where you can no longer grow. I hope you step into circles where you feel seen, where love speaks louder than anything else. Where hugs instead of handshakes are natural, even among strangers. I hope you love yourself so well that even when others don't, it doesn't sting like it used to. I hope your feet carry you to places where you feel held even when you don't feel whole. So I'll say it again, I hope you stop standing in places where you can no longer grow. And when you do, I hope that you know that an ending is also a beginning.

go where you can grow

thank you for
reading with me

About me

People always ask me how I got into writing, but I have always been a writer. I even worked as a "journalist" for the school newspaper when I was in the fifth grade. But when it comes to poetry, I started out writing lyrics, playing and singing songs I wrote on my guitar when I was fifteen. When I got married at twenty-three the music and the words stopped until I was about thirty and I started writing again. This time without the music. I kept writing through trying to heal a marriage that was never really whole, a separation, and divorce.

I started sharing what I wrote on Instagram and people asked when I was going to publish a poetry book.

So I did. Then I published another.

My books focus on self-discovery, self-love, self-healing, and finding magic in everyday, ordinary stories.

I hope you find yourself in these pages.

love,

alisha

about the book

Made of Earth is where Still Growing Wildflowers and
The Lovers meet. She's a narrative collection of poetry
and prose that shows us that even though we may have
fractured connections with our mothers and fathers,
we can find self-love and self-healing in ourselves and
our connection to our mother earth and break the
cycles of our past for our future sons and daughters.

the womb is where it begins; from the roots. This
section highlights how our childhood
relationships and experiences with our parents
shape our future relationships.

unearth / rebirth highlights toxic relationship patterns and uprooting the old belief systems and cycles that we learned from the womb. It is also a revival of the womb; a celebration of learning to accept love and give healthy love not just to others, but to ourselves.

the remedy is the hope and healing that comes from our connection to mother earth and being true to our authentic selves.

Share this book with someone who needs to hear it or share your favorite poem on Instagram and tag me @whereshegrows #madeofearth

other books

still
growing
wildflowers

Still Growing Wildflowers gives voice to past
trauma and shows you that you're still growing
wildflowers

the lovers

The Lovers is the poetry book that leads you
through a journey of self love and self healing
after heartbreak.

Made in the USA
Las Vegas, NV
15 September 2024